CRYSTAL SUCCESS

USING **CRYSTALS** FOR PERSONAL SUCCESS

Saantis Fenmu Davis

Copyright © 2022 Saantis Fenmu Davis.

All rights reserved. No part of this book may be reproduced, stored, or transmitted by any means—whether auditory, graphic, mechanical, or electronic—without written permission of both publisher and author, except in the case of brief excerpts used in critical articles and reviews. Unauthorized reproduction of any part of this work is illegal and is punishable by law.

For More Products & Services Please Visit:

SFDWELLNESS.COM

Please Follow Us At:

Facebook.com/saantisdavis

facebook.com/sfdwellness

instagram.com/saantisdavis

CONTENTS

Acknowledgments v
About the Author vii
Foreword ix

Chapter 1   Energy, The Foundation of Life 1
Chapter 2   The Power of Colors 5
Chapter 3   Crystal's, Storage of Energy 11
Chapter 4   Astrology, the study of our inner solar system 13
Chapter 5   The Seven Planetary Personas 15
Chapter 6   Lunar profile 19
Chapter 7   Mars Profile 23
Chapter 8   Mercury Profile 27
Chapter 9   Saturn Profile 31
Chapter 10 Jupiter Profile 35
Chapter 11 Venus Profile 41
Chapter 12 Solar Profile 45
Chapter 13 Basic Crystals to Have 49
Chapter 14 Crystal Care 54

ACKNOWLEDGMENTS

This book was created by me, but my village created me. I thank the Creator for giving me these abilities to help others, and those who brought me into the village, my father Tut Ner Amuf (William Davis), and mother Seshmi Khatam. Mom, I love you and appreciate you nurturing my dreams. A mother's love is unconditional. Dad, I know you are watching over me and leading me in the right direction. Thank you and I hope this book and all my work in the future do your legacy justice. You taught me how to be a man of the people and dedicated my life to the upliftment of mankind. I love you. To my kids and the rest of my family, thank you for all the support you have given to me to get me where I am today.

My gratitude goes to the mentors who inspired me, taught me, molded me, and pushed me to be better. First, I want to thank Shekhem Ur Shekhem, Ra Un Nefer Amen. I could not have accomplished this without the spiritual foundation you laid down. Ohene Nana Tuda, Uraua Hehi Metu Ra En Khamit, Nana Asadu, Raminyah Ingram, Iyanla Vanzant, Seshemsa Aakhut, Chris Holder, Momma Lori, John E Maxwell, Dr. S Ama Wrey, Baba Ras Ben, Queen Afua, thank you for inspiring me, pushing me, guiding me, being an example of success, and living your calling with class and fearlessness.

A special thanks to the village: Ausar Auset, Asante Nkonim Kurom, my music family, P.A.S.C.E.P. family, and the social media family as well as everyone who has poured into the cup that is me.

ABOUT THE AUTHOR

Saantis Davis, born in Philadelphia, is a transformational author, educator, and counselor. He has been a student of the spiritual and healing arts since he was a child. He has over fifteen years of experience in these healing arts and is the author of the book "Happiness is an Inside Job"

Certified in Music and Sound therapy, meditation by the City College of New York, and crystal therapy by the Dr. Karen E. Wells Academy in the U.K. In 2018, Saantis opened SFD Wellness, a company devoted to offering the tools people need to create the happiness and success they desire. As a certified crystal healer, he counsels individuals on how to use crystals and gems to assist with accomplishing goals such as healing, improving finances, and other situations. Using his over fifteen years of incorporating crystals into his daily life and collection of over two hundred different stones, he shares his talents from a place of love and servitude for the greater community and the world.

FOREWORD

I wrote this book to unite. Unite the physical and metaphysical. Unite the different areas of energy studies that most think are different things but different perspectives of the same thing. Unite the different cultural expressions. We see that the names may differ but energy is universal. Energy is the underlying principle of life. It connects us all regardless of study, religion, denomination, or mindset. We all need energy. We all want to create, attract and enjoy positive energy. We want the energy in our relationships, career, and any endeavor we are going into to have the correct energy. After years of studying crystals, I came to the clarity that I was not studying crystals, rocks, minerals, and so forth but instead I was studying energy. Crystals are nature's storage units for energy. Crystals when used right can give us that added energy to accomplish what we need to accomplish. Help us tap deeper into the energies we need at a specific time. We might need to be charismatic. We might need to be emotionally attentive. We might need to be stoic. We might need to be receptive or aggressive or compassionate. Crystals can help us tap deeper into these. I have used crystals, studied crystals, and prescribed crystals for over a decade. I have experienced the benefits of crystals and I want everyone who uses them to experience this. Learning in school, training at sports, birthing a child, presenting to investors, communicating with your loved one, or any other situation; there is a crystal for it. Enjoy this information and I wish you success on your journey of happiness and success.

CHAPTER ONE

ENERGY, THE FOUNDATION OF LIFE

To get to the root of crystals and all that is a part of this subject, we must first speak of the roots of what crystals are themselves. They are storage units of energy. Energy is the theme of life. Food is the transfer of energy from the sun to plants and animals, and then to people. Human relationships are the transfer of energy from one person to another. Even on a molecular level, atoms share electrons (energy) with other atoms. Energy is the key to life. Our ancestors on earth understood this. In today's world, the ancient understanding of energy is making a comeback. Energy has become a very active topic. People are now looking at life from an energy perspective.

We observe energy in specific fields. Yoga and Qi Gong are examples of manipulating energy through breath and movement. Cupping and Acupuncture are examples of manipulating energy through heat, cups, needles, or hands to heal. Even Western medicine has relatively new fields like Bioenergetics which study the biochemistry of humans to energy. Crystals therapy is another field that is making a comeback. Crystal therapy is the use of minerals and elements from the earth to shift your energy to heal, create and problem-solve.

Yes, crystals are beautiful to see and collect. They are very decorative. I have over two hundred plus different stones and I love how they look around my house. Beyond their beauty, however, they can be used more deeply and functionally.

We can use them to assist our kids in their education. We can use them to assist us in healing from illness. We can use them to assist us in working out at the gym or in giving confidence in a presentation at work. We can even use them for inspiration in starting a business or writing a book (I am a crystal client myself). These are just some of the many things that we can do with them. I know from experience. I am a second-generation crystal enthusiast. I was taught by legends like Baba Ras Ben, Judy Hall and so many more, many of whom have certifications in Crystal Therapy.

Since I was a kid, I have used crystals. I use and prescribe crystals to my family and clients. I have seen the results of giving certain stones to children to carry at school or to a client with writer's block. Crystals are tools that have helped me in my journey of success, and I attribute that to a solid foundation of energy. To use crystals effectively in our life journey, we must have a clear understanding of energy. In this book, we will learn an understanding of energy and an organizational structure to use crystals in our day-to-day life.

So what is energy? It has so many names when you look through different cultures and religions. Qi, Ra, Kundalini, Vitality, Life Force, Prana, Juju, Aura to name a few. At its essence, energy is animating life force. It's our libido, our energy (power) to accomplish our goals physically and spiritually.

Lifeforce aka energy is a neutral force. It is neither positive nor negative. It cannot be created or destroyed, but it can be manipulated and altered. There are several ways to change manipulate our energy. Food, diet, medicine, and herbs are the main way to affect our energy. This can consist of cleaning up our diet to unlock trapped energy or eating specific herbs and foods to stimulate a certain organ energy system. This is done medically in traditional Chinese medicine, Ayurvedic medicine, herbalism, and homeopathy. Movement is another great way to adjust our energy. Kundalini yoga, weight lifting, dance, and Qi Gong are a few examples of movement systems used to manipulate our energy.

Another way to alter or manipulate our energy is with our thoughts. This can be done through hypnosis, meditation, and other ways to program thoughts. In Chinese medicine, they say the "Yi" moves the chi. We know that chi or qi is our life force. Yi is the Chinese word for thought/think/intention. We experience a phenomenon of thought elevating qi when we think about things such as a vacation, our favorite food, or seeing a special someone, and our energy rises. We also see this when we think about a loved one who has transitioned or a traumatic situation. Our energy completely shifts. Crystal therapy, massage, and acupuncture are supplemental ways to shift energy.

All of these are different ways to explain work with energy but when you study them they all come back to the Father of energy, the sun. The sun is the first provider of energy. This is why the ancient

Egyptian word "Ra" symbolized life force and the sun. The sun provides a life force for all living things. The sun is food for plants, vitamins for animals and humans, a force that stirs the seas, and an element that heats the earth. The heat, light, radiation are forms of energy that the sun gives off that creates the stones we use in crystal therapy.

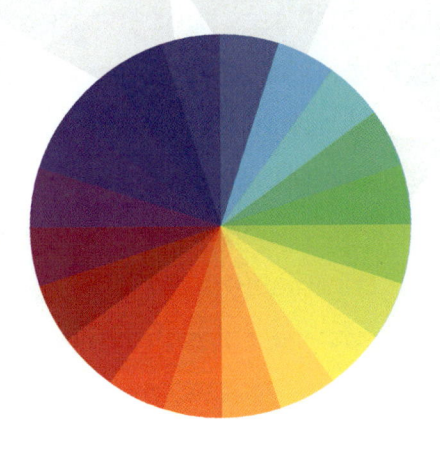

CHAPTER **TWO**

THE POWER OF COLORS

What is the significance of firefighters wearing red and police officers wearing blue? Why did they choose to make cabs, school buses, and other special vehicles yellow? Scientists have long believed that color can dramatically affect moods, feelings, emotions, and thoughts. Color is a powerful tool and can be used to influence mood, mindset, and actions. Color is light in a specific wavelength.

The specific wavelength that is represented in the crystal's color gives off a certain radiance. The wavelength aka color of the crystal gives different effects on being. This is the origin of crystal therapy. To truly understand crystal therapy, we must know Color therapy, which is also known as Chromopathy or Chromotherapy. Color therapy is an alternative therapy that uses light and its frequencies(colors) to heal physical and emotional problems. The goal of Color therapy is to correct physiological and psychological imbalances. This wisdom is based on the understanding that colors create electrical impulses in our brains that stimulate hormonal and biochemical processes in our body, calm the body or stimulate us.

Colors can influence mood, calm the nervous system and make the environment less agitating and more peace-inducing. Many cultures across the world have employed Color therapy for their healing. Even today, Chromotherapy is an essential tool for energy manipulation. Here are the primary colors we all know and their effect on our energy:

HEALING COLORS:

1. Red

Red is a color that induces vitality and stimulates energy. It increases adrenaline, blood, and heart circulation. In certain African cultures, red symbolizes heroism. It is one of the best colors for enhancing sexual appetite and overall vitality. Red also attracts attention. It is the second most visible color, which is why it is used on fire engines and stop signs to trigger alertness.

2. Orange

This engaging color represents cheer, vitality, and excitement. Orange, the color, comes from the fruit, which is packed with powerful anti-oxidants and has been known to boost immunity. It is also the most popular color among children. It is also an extroverted color. The color stands out, so it is used for safety, hunting, and construction.

3. Yellow

In the spectrum of healing colors, yellow is the brightest and represents sunshine, happiness, and joy. Yellow is the most visible color in the spectrum because the human eye processes yellow before any other color. This is why yellow is the universal color for warning signs. Yellow is a bright and cheerful color that sparks creativity to break a person out of sluggishness or lethargy.

4. Green

Green is regarded as the color of growth, rebirth, and fertility as well as freshness and harmony. It is also considered the color for bringing luck (good or bad). It is an incredibly soothing color used for healing and pregnancy.

5. Blue

The blue color is associated with calm and serenity. Blues also convey a sense of trust, loyalty, cleanliness, and understanding. Blue is a relaxing color for the mind and the body. It is nature's color for water and the sky. It is cold, wet, and slow as compared to red's warmth, fire, and intensity. Shades of blue also have very distinct properties. Dark blue symbolizes trust, dignity, intelligence, and authority. Bright blue symbolizes cleanliness, strength, calmness, serenity, and coolness. These meanings derive from the qualities of water and the ocean. (Sky) light blue evokes peace, serenity, delicateness, lightness, spirituality, understanding. These meanings are derived from the intangible aspects of the sky.

6. Pink

Pink is a soothing color that is associated with caring and affection. It is a protective and calming color. It is also a color of love, self-love, compassion, and nurturing.

7. Purple

It has been said that the color purple, as well as its related shades, like lilac, lavender, and violet, provide spiritual guidance. Purple is also associated with higher consciousness and spiritual awareness. It is also associated with power, both earthly and spiritual.

8. Black

It absorbs all of the light in the color spectrum. Black is slow, lethargic. It lacks energy. Black is used as a symbol of death (lacking energy). Having the characteristics of purple, black represents power both spiritually and earthly.

9. White

White is the father color; for it is all colors, It is the only color in total balance and harmony. It is the color of peace, beginnings, light, purity, and nothingness.

After looking at these color healing descriptions we can see the proof that colors affect us in everyday life. Psychologists, marketing executives, healers, and leaders alike use this information to shape the world.

After reading the description for red we can then understand why firemen wear red. When we understand Color therapy then we see why specific things are the color they are. Why is lapis is blue and has the effect it has, why garnet is red and has the effect it has, why rose quartz is pink and has the effect it has, and so on.

To reduce suicide rates on Tokyo's Yamanote railway line, color therapy was used in 2009. One of the worst places for suicides to occur in Tokyo was the Yamanote railway. Platforms were equipped with blue lights. As a healing color, blue is associated with calm and serenity.

The number of suicides fell by 74 percent at the stations where blue lights were installed after lights were installed. Light therapy has also been installed in other places, such as Gatwick Airport train platforms.

This is scientific proof of color therapy. When I started getting into crystals and what each one does, I started to see the effects of crystals could be organized by stone color. I saw a pattern that bluish greenish crystals (turquoise, chrysoprase, chrysocolla, amazonite) worked in assisting in healing, fertility, transformation, and creating. I saw there was a pattern of what black stones did for energy. They all had the purpose of use for spiritual work(obsidian, onyx, marinate, black jasper, black opal, jet, and more). I can go on with more colors and stone. This cannot be a coincidence. Nature makes no coincidences. This is science. The colors are beautiful and marvelous to look at but their color is also a gateway to therapy.

CHAPTER **THREE**

CRYSTAL'S, STORAGE OF ENERGY

Crystals and their colors are influenced by factors such as heat, light, and radiation from the sun, elements and minerals found in the area, and temperature. Sodalite and lapis are very similar but the addition of copper in the environment creates lapis. The color of amethyst is violet when it is exposed to solar radiation and iron impurities are added. In essence, this information shows us that that they are all mini storage units for specific energy, elements, and minerals of the sun. Through these energies, we can influence our own. This is possible because we are also on a greater level, storage units of energy. We are energy beings. In our lives, we have to be able to shift our energy to whatever is needed in the situation for success. We have careers, relationships, children, and other positions that need us to express a certain style of energy. Later in the book we will find that we have a multitude of energy personas inside of us. We need all of them to create the success we desire in our lives. If we try to operate in with only one expression of energy, we create a lifestyle where we succeed in certain areas and crash and burn in others. We must become adaptable, multiple, adjustable in our energies. Crystals can assist with this process. Crystals will give us a specific energy boost. Let's say for example I know I must boost my solar energy to be successful. Stones like ruby and garnet, as well as metal gold, will help me shift my energy to that specific wavelength, just as mantras and meditation work to cultivate and stimulate that solar energy.

In the ancient language of Sanskrit, ruby is called Ratnaraj, or "King of precious stones." and was worn by many leaders (the popes, pharaohs, kings in Europe) because of its effect of making a person feel powerful, vital, courageous and strong. The background history of a ruby is a testament to its functional use for leaders of all sizes and staturecusing ruby. The evolution of how we carry these batteries of nature keeps innovating. People carry crystals in so many ways. I am a traditionalist so I still carry stones in my pocket like people in the old times. Now people are purchasing crystals in the form of sculpted art, furniture, house items like chinaware, bowls, lamps, and more. I have met an educator who has a chair made of lapis in his study room. We will also see crystals being cut and forged into jewelry and even clothes. Rings, necklaces, earrings, bracelets, waist beads, anklets and many other items are being made with crystals to use their energy. Face rollers, yoni eggs, acupuncture point tools and the list goes on. Humans will keep creating new ways to carry nature's energy.

CHAPTER **FOUR**

ASTROLOGY, THE STUDY OF OUR INNER SOLAR SYSTEM

What exactly is astrology? Essentially, astrology is the study of the energy of the planet. It is the study of earth's planetary energy, its patterns, and relationships to other planets. This study is important since the energy radiating from the earth impacts us greatly. A basic example of the earth's change in energy affecting us is in the seasons.

It is based on the earth's relationship with the sun. During the summer, the Northern Hemisphere points at the sun, so we have the longest amount of daylight (energy), almost fourteen hours on the longest day. This high amount of heat/light energy is why we are the most active and have the most vitality in the summer. We are feeding off the extra boost of energy from the sunlight.

During the winter, there are fewer hours of daylight in the Northern Hemisphere, which reduces the amount of heat energy we receive. This decrease in heat energy affects us.

This is why people feel less energetic, motivated and have less vitality. "Winter Blues", depression, and other conditions are linked to this time of the year. It's directly connected to the amount of energy the earth offers us.

The solar system also has other planets such as Mars, Venus, Jupiter, and so on that create changes on the earth based on their movement. I won't go too deep into astrology. That could be a separate book. This chapter is to show that astrology is one of the background components to the science of crystal healing and also our everyday life.

CHAPTER FIVE

THE SEVEN PLANETARY PERSONAS

Astrology teaches that when you are born, the planets' alignments affect you. Each of us possesses all seven planetary personas inside of us. The time of birth, therefore, dictates the dominant and dormant energies that reside within us. Persona is a Greek word that refers to a character.

The word character means distinct qualities. Each planet has its expression. These expressions show emotional, behavioral, cognitive characteristics that we display in all aspects of our lives. These are called personality traits. An example of this is the lunar planetary persona. This persona expresses its energy in the qualities of nurturing, caring, sensitivity, yielding, etc. We exhibit these qualities in our lives when we are in the positions of parents, spouses, caretakers, nurses, healers, therapists, spouses, and so on.

To reach our goals in life we must strengthen and purify these seven planetary energies within us so that we have access to them and can call forth whichever energy is needed for success at that time.

We can use crystals to assist with improving the energy within us.

All seven energies within us are not present from birth. That is why life experiences can help us develop all seven energies. You may ask "where do crystals fit into this picture". Crystals are thumb drives of stored energy.

We can leverage the energy within them to assist us in shifting to another persona and getting deeper into the persona.

Within each planetary persona, are dozens of stones that serve different purposes. In my next book, I will describe the functions of each stone. In this book, we will lay out the method for combining an understanding of seven planets with our success.

The original seven planets we are using are the sun, moon, mars, mercury, Jupiter, Venus, and Saturn.

They are referred to as the old planets because they are visible to the naked eye. There are seven planets and personas, corresponding to the seven days of the week. In many cultures, each day is devoted to one of those planets and their personas or a god, energy, etc.

Sunday: This comes from the Old English word, Sunnandeag, meaning "Day of the Sun." This is based on Germanic mythology of the god of the sun named Sunna or Sól in Roman. In other cultures, this day refers to Heru, Micha-El, Bhuvaneshvari, St Barbara, Shango, Jakuta, Tipareth, and Jesus.

Monday: Monday gets its name from the Anglo-Saxon word "Mondandaeg" which translates to "The Moon's Day." It's also tied to the planet moon as shown in the name for Monday as Spanish Lunes (lunar). In other cultures, this day refers to Auset, Mary, Yemaya, Dhumavati, Yesod, Gabri-el, Our Lady of Regla.

Tuesday: Tuesday is named after Tiwes or Tyr, the Nordic god of war. This day is named after the Germanic god Tyr. The Germanic peoples adopted the Roman weekly calendar and replaced the names of the Roman god Mars (Aries, the Greek god name is one of Mars' zodiac signs) with Tyr. The planet for Tuesday is Mars and Tuesday in Latin is called "Martis dies" which means "Mars's Day". In other cultures this day refers to Ogun, Bagalamukhi, Khama-El, Geburah, St Peter, and Herukhuti.

Wednesday: It is named after the Germanic god, Woden. This day is named after the Germanic god, Thor. The Germanic peoples adopted the Roman weekly calendar and replaced the names of Roman gods (mercury) with Woden. The planet for this day is mercury. Wednesday is Mercredi in French, Miercuri in Romanian, and Miercoles in Spanish. In other cultures, this day refers to St. Anthony, Rapha-El, Elegba, Eshu, Matangi, Hod, Sebek, Anpu, and Apuat.

Thursday: This day is named after the Germanic god Thor. The Germanic peoples adopted the Roman weekly calendar and replaced the names of Roman gods (Jupiter) with Thor. Dies Iovis ('day of Jupiter') is how Thursday is known in Latin. Jupiter is the planet associated with Thursday. In other cultures, this day refers to Saggitarius: Orunmila, St. Francis of Assisi, Chinnamasta, Ifa, Ratzi-El, Chokmah, Tehuti Pisces: Maat, Lakshmi, Aje Chagullia, Gedulah, Chesed, Tzadki-El, and Seshat.

Friday: The name Friday is the Germanic word meaning the "Day of Frige", named after the Goddess Frige. The Germanic people adopting the Roman calendar replaced the Roman goddess Venus with Frige. In the language of Latin, dies Veneris means "day of (the planet) Venus,".

In other cultures, this day refers to Het Heru, Neb-Het, Hana-El, Oshun, Kamalatmika, and Lady of Charity of Cobre, Netzach.

Saturday: Named after the Roman god and planet Saturn, Saturday is the only day of the week that retained its Roman origin till this day. In other cultures, this day refers to Kali, St. Lazarus, Babalu Aye, Binah, Tzaphki-El, Ama, Aima, Seker, Ptah, Aummit, and Khepere.

You will see this system integrates into other cultures (Kemetic, Akan, Yoruba, Catholic, etc.) Understanding these seven energy profiles is to know oneself better. All seven of these energies exist within each of us. Some may be dominant, while others may be dormant, but the key to success in life is to cultivate and grow each one within us to become more balanced and whole.

CHAPTER **SIX**

LUNAR PROFILE

Significators

Planet: Moon
Day: Monday
Gem Colors: blue family, blue/green combination, white
Number: 7
Chakra: Visarga
Astrology signs: Cancer
Angels: Auset, Mary, Yemaya, Dhumavati, Yesod, Gabri-el, Our lady of Regla, Adwoa/Adwo
Herbalism: Spearmint, Lettuce, Purslane, Jasmine,

Stones

chrysocolla   amazonite   moonstone   turquoise

Traits

Caring, conservative, benevolent, accommodating, sweet mannered, timorous, comfort-loving, wanting security, to be free of difficulties, daydreaming, receptiveness, memory, transformation, reflection, risk assessing, humility, yielding, devotion, trance, meditation.

Careers:

- Positions that require emotional sensitivity and receptivity: child care, social worker, nurse, teachers of kids, positions that deal with healing/ transformation: doctors, midwives, counselors, nurse
- positions that nurture others: assistants, health aid, chef, farmers, servants, domestic life, parents, millers, dealers, and workers of food and liquid
- Early childhood education.

Biological Info

- Physiology: the well-being of the reproductive organs, digestion, autonomous nervous system, assimilative.

- Pathology: infertility, menstrual problems, digestive problems, catarrhal conditions, chlorosis, anemia, edema, dropsy
- Therapeutics: alternative, diuretic, nutrient.

Energy Overview

Lunar energy deals with our development. It deals with the assimilation process in the mind and digestion. It is the receptive part of us where we learn and program our minds. We can also change our programming using trance, via meditation. This process of using trance to change our programming is referred to as transformation.

When we unite our will (clear specific images of what we would like to accomplish) with our life force (energy in motion, emotion) in the body through meditation (trance), we create the devotion and motivation to achieve our goals. We must be clear on what emotions are and how to make use of them so we maximize them. We are energy beings aka life forms. Emotion is our energy, life force, chi.

The amount of energy we have and how it is flowing is what we mean by our emotional state. When we are happy, our energy is high and flowing, which makes us feel empowered. Our energy level is low when we are depressed or gloomy. When our energy level is low and stagnant, we are fearful and feel powerless. Our energy level is the key to our success.

We must also know the role of emotions. They are to energize our will. What we must know is that emotions' job is not to guide the will. The will must be guided by wisdom(sages, intuitive faculties, ancestors, elders, experts, readings). Once we have received direction and declared with our will then we must energize that declaration through meditation. This is the role of our emotions.

CHAPTER SEVEN

MARS PROFILE

Significators

Planet: Mars
Day: Tuesday
Gem Colors: red family
Number: 11
Chakra: Indu
Astrology signs: Aries, Scorpio
Angels: Ogun, Bagalamukhi, Khama-El, Geburah, St Peter, Herukhuti, Bena/Abenaa,
Herbalism: Pine, Cedarwood, tobacco, holly(Quita maldicion), Anamu, Rompe Saraguey.

Stones

garnet *fire agate* *red aventurine* *carnelian*

Traits

Courageous, fearless, not afraid of bodily harm, energetic, prudent, forceful, enterprising, magnanimous, forceful, constructive, muscularly skillful, zealous, passionate, delighted and motivated by challenges or hard and dangerous (short)work, blunt, trailblazing, detachment, initiative, confidence, drive, physical power.

Careers:

- positions that require fearlessness(high risk): fighters, soldiers, firemen, cops, hunters, people employed in dangerous undertakings, athletes, competitive, butchers, surgeons,
- positions that deal with enforcement of rules: cops, debt collectors, bounty hunters, criminal lawyers, prosecutors, inspectors,
- positions that require analysis: business executive, analytical theoreticians, stockbroker, mechanic
- Positions of high physical labor, highly competitive work.

Biological Info

- Physiology: The immune system, voluntary musculature, elimination of toxins through the skin, focused heat production, sexual excitement.

- Pathology: Acute disorders (fevers, inflammations, eruptive infections), wounds(from weapons), burns, hemorrhage, blood/skin disorders(itching, hot, eczemas, poxes, etc), ruptures, injuries, accidents.
- Therapeutics: surgery, stimulants, tonics, aphrodisiacs, resolvents, caustic, rubefacient, and vesicant.

Energy Overview

The Martian energy profile deals with confidence. One of the most important keys to our success is courage. The courage to live a life free from fear. Fear is false evidence masquerading as truth. Essentially, we are being told that if we act or do not act, something in the past will happen again or something in the future will not occur.

Although we think this feeling serves us, it does not. We let our past or future dictate the current now. We go into a relationship and because the person reminds you of a previous relationship that was sour, we don't give this one person the fair shake they deserve.

In our careers, we select based on how our parents will view our choices in the future. We avoid taking risks now due to possible failure in the future. Every one of us has in our lives experiences that have challenged us to grow, develop, and change. We are born with all of the tools, in our spirits, we need to manage every situation we encounter. Money, "The Man", your boss at work, this relationship, or any other external factor isn't what you need to become successful.

It is our lack of self-confidence that weakens us. Internal doubt saps our ability to carry out tasks. Fear does not safeguard us. It is only when we let go of this idea that opportunities open up, healing occurs and growth occurs.

CHAPTER EIGHT

MERCURY PROFILE

Significators

Planet: Mercury
Day: Wednesday
Gem Colors: yellow, brown, orange
Number: 3
Chakra: Manas
Astrology signs: Gemini, Virgo
Angels: St. Anthony, Rapha-El, Elegba, Eshu, Matangi, Hod, Sebek, Anpu, Apuat, Awuku/Akua
Herbalism: Oregano, Lavender, Larkspur, Lilly of the Valley, Abre Camino, Arrasa Con Todo

Stones

yellow opal   *yellow apatite*   *chalcopyrite*

Traits

Sharp and witty, fond of traveling, critical in a positive way, able to separate issues based on external, loquacious, diplomatic, cold and pedantic, communicative, dependent on information(data), perception, segregative thinking, syllogistical, logical, labeling, defining or giving meaning.

Careers:

Positions that require oratorial skills: public speakers, diplomats, politicians, preachers, trial lawyer, debater, teachers, opinionated speaking jobs, positions that deal with information(data) gathering or disseminating: journalist, talk radio, announcer, (speaker for a king, president or important person), office workers, students, clerks, master of ceremonies, positions that require logistical skill: mathematicians, technicians, astrologers, schemers, traders,

Biological Info

› Physiology: The immune system, voluntary musculature, elimination of toxins through the skin, focused heat production, sexual excitement.

- Pathology: Acute disorders (fevers, inflammations, eruptive infections), wounds(from weapons), burns, hemorrhage, blood/skin disorders(itching, hot, eczemas, poxes, etc), ruptures, injuries, accidents.
- Therapeutics: surgery, stimulants, tonics, aphrodisiacs, resolvents, caustic, rubefacient, and vesicant.

Energy Overview

Mercury is the element associated with perception. We must realize that how we see ourselves and what we experience determines the reality in which we operate. We label everything in life by our perception. Our lives are full of experiences, and we have been taught that these experiences define us, but life shows us that no experience has a quality necessarily, that quality comes from the individual.

Five adults can lose their job and experience five different results. Here are three different responses to the same loss of job scenario. One can become an entrepreneur, another can learn to be a better employee, and another can become depressed and lose their identity.

So is being fired from a job good or bad? A job loss is whatever you label it to be. The power of perception or labeling is divine power.

Life experiences are not pre-determined but self-determined. Life experiences do not define us, but rather how we define the experience makes that determination.

CHAPTER NINE
SATURN PROFILE

Significators

Planet: Saturn
Day: Saturday
Gem Colors: black, dark blue
Number: 13
Chakra: Nirvana
Astrology sign: Capricorn, Aquarius
Angels: Kali, St. Lazarus, Babalu Aye, Binah, Tzaphki-El, Ama, Aima, Seker, Ptah, Aummit, Khepere, Amen Men/Amenmenawaa.
Herbalism: Jerusalem Tea, Bitter Broom, Myrrh, Cypress, Southernwood Leaves, Artemisia, Vulgaris

Stones

black onyx   *obsidian*   *amethyst*   *shungite*

Traits

Stable, sober, steadfast, reserved in speech, thrifty, studious, austere, steadfast in friendship, reliable, appreciative of structure, limitations, patient, hard-working, organized, methodical,

Careers

Undertakers, priest, positions that work with the earth: farmers, miners, subway workers, geographers, organizers, positions that deal with structure or organizing: project planner, architect, etc, businesses or jobs that deal in long term returns and take long term work: real estate owner, long term stocks, etc.

Biological Info

- Physiology: Skeletal system, catabolism, aging, crystallizing functions of the body.
- Pathology: Abnormal depositions of crystallized materials (gallstones, kidney stones, etc), an abnormal amount of uric acid, gout, rheumatoid arthritis, deep-seated disorders, paralysis, sclerosis, blood impurities.
- Therapeutics: Healing thru incantations, refrigerants, hypnagogic, styptics, astringents, antipyretics.

Energy Overview

The Saturn energy profile reminds us that life is masterfully ordered. That implies that, first of all, all experiences (people, places, things) we have are not random but have been destined to be in our lives. All experiences in our life are to move us to our calling (our specific divine purpose).

Earth has a life cycle called seasons. Plants have a life cycle, and our bodies have a life cycle. Our spiritual journey also has a life cycle. We grow at times, stand still (rest) at others, and weaken at others. It is nothing to fear.

In essence, the experiences are to encourage growth, and the decay(material loss, character change, change) that we have in our lives is the release of things that no longer serve us in our journey moving forward. Therefore, it is not a true loss.

CHAPTER TEN

JUPITER PROFILE

Significators

SAGITTARIUS BIO

Planet: Jupiter
Day: Thursday
Gem Colors: blue family
Number: 8
Chakra: Guru
Astrology signs: Saggitarius
Angels: Orunmila, St. Francis of Assisi, Chinnamasta, Ifa, Ratzi-El, Chokmah, Tehuti, Ywa/Yaa/Aaba
Herbalism: Lotus, Sweet Almond, Thuja

Stones

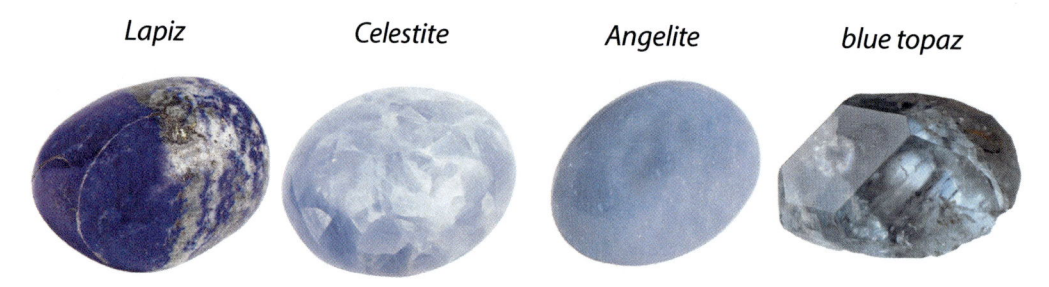

Lapiz   Celestite   Angelite   blue topaz

Traits

Just minded, equilibrated, holistic, generous, sharing, optimistic, liberal, magnanimous, moral sense, positively striving for advancement and wealth, religious, "fortunate", law-abiding, fair, charitable, grateful, prudent, deferring to elders, big picture thinking, abundant minded, theoretical, unifying,

Careers

Positions that give wisdom: priest and priestesses, spiritual leaders, sages, experts in a field, teachers at the highest levels, scientists, lawyers, officials, theoreticians, theologians, positions that work with high finance: banker, merchant.

Biological Info

- Physiology: the conservation, preservation, and expansion of the life force. The liver, production and storage of blood sugar(glycogenesis), breakdown of protein waste into urea, the creation and regulation of sex hormones, arterial circulation, and arterial blood.
- Pathology: accumulation of protein in the blood, waste in the blood, liver derangements, sthenic plethora, localized swelling, accumulation of adipose tissue, adipose sarcoma, lardaceous, solenoid cancer of the mammary, pancreatic glands, vascular congestion leading to hemorrhages, apoplexy, epistaxis, fatty degeneration, diabetes, illnesses of pleasurable access(diet, sex, etc)

- Therapeutics: joy, analeptic, alternative, nurturing, spermatogenic, emollient, fattening, equilibrating, anabolic, promoter(steroids, etc)
- Chinese Medicine: Liver/gall Bladder system, damp disease pattern, herbs that clear heat and disperse dampness(artemisia capillaris, minor bupleurum, pulsatilla, eight correction powder, etc)

Energy Overview

Sagittarius is the energy of truth, the basis for our thinking, feeling, and acting. It represents the universal laws of spirit (qi, energy, etc.).

These are the premises that energy works off of. When we know and operate in line with these premises the internal knowledge aka intuition will flow through us.

The experts we need will appear. We can live a life of peace and joy, we can accomplish goals. This is why it is said that knowledge is power. Not just any knowledge but knowledge of the spirit!

Significators　　　　　　　　　　　　　　**PISCES BIO**

Planet: Jupiter
Day: Thursday
Gem Colors: Blue Family, Yellow
Number:
Chakra: Indu(Pisces)
Astrology signs: Pisces
Angels: Maat, Lakshmi, Aje Chagullia, Gedulah, Chesed, Tzadki-El, Seshat,
Herbalism: Thuja, Anise, Oak Moss, Aloes, Honeysuckle

Stones

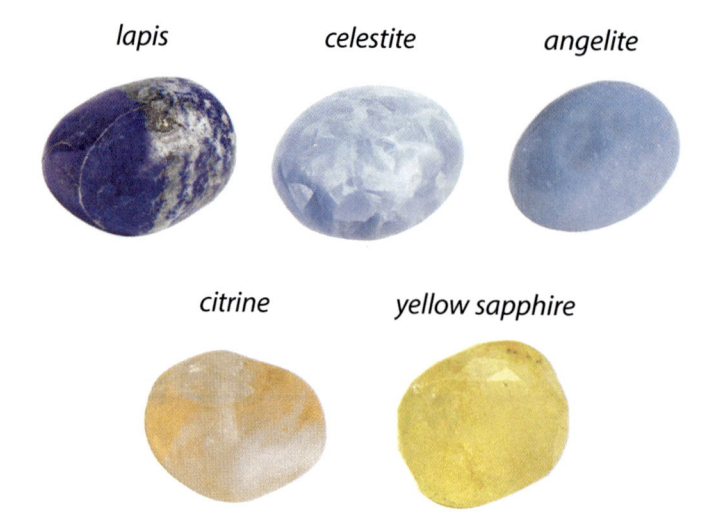

lapis *celestite* *angelite*

citrine *yellow sapphire*

Traits

Just, equilibrated, holistic, generous, sharing, optimistic, liberal, magnanimous, moral sense, positively striving for advancement and wealth, religious, "fortunate", law-abiding, fair, charitable, grateful, prudent, deferring to elders, big picture thinking, abundant minded, theoretical, unifying,

Careers

Lawyers, theoretical scientists, bankers, priests, government officials, merchants, theologians, managers, high tenured priests and priestesses, teachers at the highest levels, scientists, theoreticians, positions that work with high finance, positions that implement laws

Biological Info

- Physiology: The conservation, preservation, and expansion of the life force. The liver, production and storage of blood sugar(glycogenesis), breakdown of protein waste into urea, the creation and regulation of sex hormones, arterial circulation, and arterial blood.

- Pathology: Accumulation of protein in the blood, waste in the blood, liver derangements, sthenic plethora, localized swelling, accumulation of adipose tissue, adipose sarcoma, lardaceous, solenoid cancer of the mammary, pancreatic glands, vascular congestion leading to hemorrhages, apoplexy, epistaxis, fatty degeneration, diabetes, illnesses of pleasurable access(diet, sec, etc)
- Therapeutics: joy, analeptic, alternative, nurturing, spermatogenic, emollient, fattening, equilibrating, anabolic, promoter(steroids, etc)
- Chinese Medicine: Liver/gall Bladder system, damp disease pattern, herbs that clear heat and disperse dampness(artemisia capillaris, minor bupleurum, pulsatilla, eight correction powder, etc)

Energy Overview

In the Jupiterian energy profile, we become aware of the underlying principles that underlie all of life. We gain a broad picture of life when we are conscious of universal spiritual laws.

Universal spiritual laws show us that all things in this universe are connected. Bees need the trees to gain nectar, the trees need the bees to spread pollen and germinate the trees, humans need the trees to breathe oxygen and the trees need us to breathe carbon dioxide. There is an intricate balance of interdependence in life.

Also in our universe, there is a delicate balance. We must make sure that we are living in harmony with those Universal Spiritual laws to have a healthy, happy, successful life. Love is another important idea of this Jupiter energy. Love is giving, seeking nothing in return(unconditional). It is the highest showing of God's energy. When we are manifesting this we move outside of the realm of self and into the universal essence.

CHAPTER ELEVEN

VENUS PROFILE

Significators

Planet: Venus
Day: Friday
Gem Colors: pink, green, yellow,
Number: 5
Chakra: Manas
Basic Gem: rose quartz, green jade, zoisite, pink opal, green aventurine, malachite
Astrology signs: Libra, Taurus
Angels: Het Heru, Neb-Het, Hana-El, Oshun, Kamalatmika, Lady of Charity of Cobre, Netzach, Afi/Fi.

> **Herbalism**: Yellow roses, Honeysuckle, Calendula Flower, Maiden's Hair, Spearmint, Sandalwood, Cinnamon, Rose, Parsley, Vetiver.

Stones

Rose quartz *green jade* *green aventurine* *pink opal*

Traits

Sociable, affectionate, pleasure-loving, harmonious, joyful, sweet, engaging, flexible, sympathetic, graceful, merry, cheerful, congregational thinking, imaginative, metaphors, myths stories to explain, creative, visionary, dreamer, enchanting, the life of the party,

Careers:

- Positions that require creativity: musician, dancer, actor, singer, entertainers, artists, painters, fashion, adornment industry(jewelry, etc), fiction/story writer, advertising, marketing,
- positions that deal with social: a person who has parties or other fun social events, public relations,

Biological Info

- Physiology: The immune system, voluntary musculature, elimination of toxins thru the skin, focused heat production, sexual excitement.
- Pathology: Illnesses of the reproductive organs, mumps, gestational problems(miscarriages), varicosities(legs, scrotum), hemorrhoids, aneurysms, renal disorders, cysts, venereal illness, laxity of fiber, tumors, asthenic plethora, stomach disorders from dietary excess.
- Therapeutics: joyful events, emetic, diuretics, demulcent, alternative/ detoxifiers.
- Chinese Medicine: Kidney/ bladder system, blood and qi disease pattern

Energy Overview

The planetary energy of Venus is associated with joy. What is joy? Joy is the feeling of aroused energy (energizing). Humans are led to believe that joy is found in people, places, and things.

However, as we walk our spiritual journey, we realize that the state of joy (enjoyment, enjoyment) is not found in the experience, but brought to the experience by the individual. Five different people can ride a roller coaster and have five different feelings about it. So can we say roller coasters are universally enjoyable? We definitely can not. We can choose to be in a joyful state or not. This understanding is liberating because when we understand that joy is an internal skill or choice. We are no longer holding our joy ransom while waiting for that relationship, item (car, money), or even goal to arrive.

Joy is also the first step in creating positive change in our lives. To achieve our goals, we need to be filled with joy. We are enthusiastic towards a goal when we feel joyous (state of joy). We all declare goals, but we never see them become a reality because we lack the motivation to keep moving forward. Imagine the goals you are passionate about achieving. Do you find it difficult to achieve them? When there is joy, there is no struggle or lack of motivation.

People can play basketball for six hours straight, work for eight hours and then go to a party for four hours, climb Mount Everest, participate in Triathlons. Different people thinking about these experiences would feel different perceptual levels of joy. Joy is experienced when it's a situation they're joyful about. That is the power of joy. This understanding also lets us see that joy isn't at the end of our goals but a vital part of reaching them. The idea of joy coming when I accomplish the goal is one of the main roadblocks that could stop you from accomplishing the goal that you truly want to accomplish.

CHAPTER TWELVE

SOLAR PROFILE

Significators

Planet: Sun
Day: Sunday
Gem Colors: red family, light red, dark red, orange
Number: 6
Chakra: Hrit
Sound: Hring
Astrology signs: Leo
Angels: Heru, Micha-El, Bhuvaneshvari, St Barbara, Shango, Jakuta, Tipareth, Awusi/Esi/Asi

> **Herbalism**: poplar leaves, paraiso, cocks comb, geranium, bay leaves, rompe saraguey (eupatorium odoratum), frankincense (olibanum)

Stones

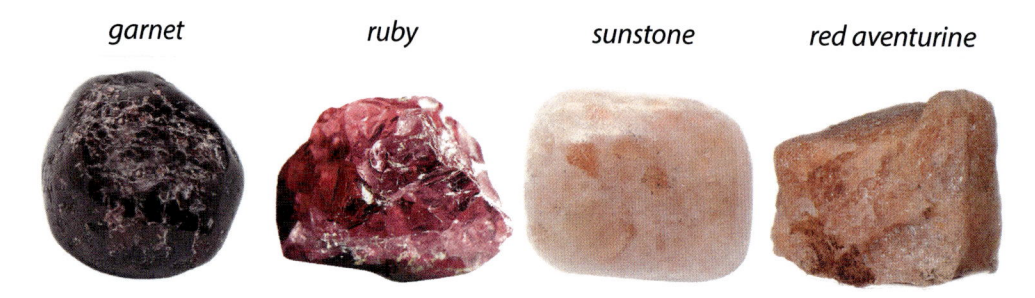

| garnet | ruby | sunstone | red aventurine |

Emotional Traits

Magnanimous, desirous of power and leadership, strong-willed, full of vitality, zealous, noble, lofty, proud, ardent, authoritative, humane, reserved, above using underhanded means versus competition, decisive, self-confident, center of the group in social settings.

Career and Functions:

Positions of leading people (leader of people), presidents, kings, mayors and governors, self-employed, head of house household, servant leadership positions, managers, coaches, mentors.

Biological Info

- Physiology: Cardiovascular system, the heart, vitality(vital energy) which comes from the sun(heat), plants receive it thru

photosynthesis; humans and animals get it from the sun and eating
- Pathology: cardiac problems, arterial circulatory problems, fevers
- Therapeutics: Cardiac, alternative, constitutional homeopathic remedies regardless of organ affinity, tonics.
- Chinese Medicine: Heart/Small intestines system, heat and fire disease pattern, detoxify and drain fire, enrichen yin(Coptis detoxifying formula, great yin pills, etc)

Energy Overview

The solar energy profile deals with our understanding and our exercising of choice. Choice is the essence of our divinity and freedom. Most spiritual and religious manuscripts say that mankind has the likeness of God, but what does that mean?

Only humans have programming, out of all the living creatures that God created, but we can also choose to ignore it or reprogram it. As a basic example, we see behavioral changes such as altering dietary habits, extreme examples such as monks setting themselves on fire and then sitting in meditation, and suicides and hunger strikes.

Suicide, the monks and hunger strikes illustrate how we can bypass the evolutionary programming of self-preservation. No other animal can do so. This is an example of our freedom or godliness. It comes with the understanding that we are responsible for the thoughts, feelings, and actions we take (what we choose).

Even though we cannot control what experiences we have, we can control how we react to them emotionally, physically, and mentally. To exhibit such control, a high level of vitality is required. One must also develop self-control. We discipline ourselves by cutting the emotional and mental attachments we have to outside things. Attachments affect the integrity of our choices by eliminating options that exist where we do not have to exist without the attachment.

As an example, we see people with lung cancer who are waiting for lung transplants yet still smoke cigarettes. If the doctors discover you are smoking, they take you off the list. Despite wanting to live, the attachment to the cigarette is compromising the right to choose to live. They are not choosing to die consciously; they lack the vitality and self-discipline to break free from the cigarettes.

CHAPTER **THIRTEEN**

BASIC CRYSTALS TO HAVE

I put together a basic tool kit that comprises of crystals from each energy profile, as well as two complementary stones. These stones cover most of the common issues we deal with, and they are readily available and cost-effective. My next book will talk about more stones and details of stones.

CRYSTAL LIST:

1. White Agate

It is a stone that encourages introspection and contemplation, boosting your spiritual awareness and giving you a sense of confidence. White agate also stabilizes energy, balancing yin and yang. It facilitates the journey of self-discovery.

2. Lapis
This stone is for the Jupitarian profile. Lapis stimulates the higher mental faculties. This stone teaches us the power of listening to divine wisdom as it reveals the inner truth. Good for mental clarity.

3. Amethyst
A Saturnian profile stone: It enhances spiritual (metaphysical) ability. The stone protects against psychic attacks. It has a stabilizing effect on the mind and energy. It helps overcome addiction (negative habits) or replace them with positive ones. Amethyst is also helpful for people about to make transitions through death and their family.

4. Citrine
It is used for Venusian goals and special objectives in the Jupitatian profile. It attracts abundance but does not attract materials. However, it gives the wearer of the stone an energy boost relative to their work. It's good for helping manifest visions. It assists in clearing out thoughts of impoverishment and stagnation. It also helps to encourage sharing with others.

Money Bowl Practice: Place citrine in a copper bowl, along with dimes, and gently rub honeysuckle oil on all the ingredients. Put your hands in the bowl each day as if you're washing your hands in money, and then rub them against your clothes. As you do this, remind yourself that your character is what will attract the resources, people, and things you need to increase your finances.

5. Garnet

Garnet is an energizing stone. It helps remove inhibitions and fears. It encourages self-confidence and courage, making it useful in times of dire need. It also is a stone for protection because it helps keep our vitality high. Our vitality is the source of our spiritual and psychic power. Vitality is also tied to our libido.

6. Ruby

Similar to garnet, ruby empowers us to walk our spiritual journey with passion. It also helps energize us and raise our vitality. It can protect us from psychic attacks, outside influences.

7. Yellow Opal

This stone is used in the Mercurian profile. Yellow opal enhances our thinking and reinforces positive thought patterns.

8. Rose Quartz

Generally speaking, rose quartz works for Venusian profiles. Rose quartz is used to cleanse, open and harmonize the Venus energy system. It promotes comradery and harmony and enhances creativity. By tapping into the emotional part of our spirit, this stone helps to release trauma and deep emotional pain.

9. Chrysocolla

In addition to being used for the lunar profile, chrysocolla is an excellent stone for transformation. It assists in making meditation deeper. Additionally, it cleanses the aura. Chrysocolla helps us to stay calm in difficult situations and helps us to remain flexible. It also helps increase our capacity to love and care.

10. Clear Quartz

Known as the crystal of power, Quartz heightens any energy/intention. When held, quartz can almost double your biomagnetic field. Acupuncturists use quartz to increase the efficiency of needles. It enhances metaphysical abilities and is a generator of electromagnetism while dispelling static electricity.

11. Celestite

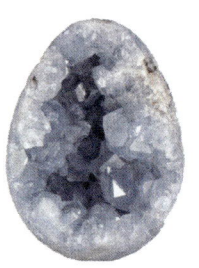

This stone is used for the Jupitarian profile. It assists in the gist of intuition and other psychic abilities. It helps us to tap into the divine wisdom of the divine (ancestors, angels, etc).

12. Moonstone

This stone is used for the lunar profile. Moonstone is used to seek the energy of the (yin) aspect of our spirit. This stone helps us to carry out transformation. It helps us to tap into the yielding, sensitive, receptive part of our being. Assisting us in the development of emotional intelligence, ties directly into the lunar qualities. It also helps us dream, meditate, visualize, and other trance states.

13. Jade

This stone is used for the Venusian profile. It is said that jade is a stone the ancients used to do magic. It nurtures the imagination and visualizations thus it is also seen as a stone of attraction. It does not attract materials but assists the person who is wearing the stone in their work to become more attractive in an energy sense. This stone will also help in building relationships and harmony in life.

14. Onyx

Ancient cultures said onyx was a stone that facilitates one's destiny. This stone aids in forming and breaking habits, structures, and formations of any sort. It is effective when used for past life work. A stone of consistency, it assists us in dealing with long hard work. It absorbs energy and assists with the transformation of energy. An assistant in the development of psychic and spiritual power.

CHAPTER FOURTEEN

CRYSTAL CARE

To maintain our crystals, it is important to be able to clean and recharge our stones. Our stones have been touched by others before you purchase them. As the crystals traveled from being mined to being in a shop, they will have absorbed multiple energies.

Many people had touched them in that process and therefore transferred their energy onto the crystal. It is vital that we cleanse them.

Whenever you purchase a stone, you want it to have only your thought intention and energies on it. There are many ways to cleanse your crystals, allowing them to be neutral. Once they are neutral, we must charge them with our own personal energy/ thought and intention. Crystals are like little energy batteries. After several uses, they must be recharged, just as your body needs food to refuel itself.

CLEANSING YOUR STONE:

1. You can burn sage and pass a crystal several times through the smoke. Sage smudging has traditionally been used to protect against negativity.
2. You can bury them in your garden for 24 - 48 hours. The crystals came from and were formed underground, and returning them to a similar environment allows them to be naturally cleansed.
3. You can cleanse crystals in running water. This can be under the tap at home or even better in a running stream. The best thing to do if you have access to a stream is to place your crystals in a small net bag which you can attach to something at the water's edge so that they don't get washed away. About 24 hours is a good period for this. Please check to see if the crystal is safe for water. (ex. Water shrinks selenite)
4. If your crystal can be heated, you can pass the crystal through the flame a few times to cleanse it. Make sure your crystal is safe to heat.
5. Your crystals can be submerged in salt. (Check to see if your crystals are salt-resistant)

ENERGIZING YOUR STONE:

As well as cleansing your crystals, they also need to be energized. Just as humans need food and water, crystals also require a charge or energy. Some of the cleansing practices also energize at the same time:

1. The main way I recommend for people to charge their crystals is with intention. This can be done through meditation, mental

seeding, and other methods when holding the crystal. Using the right energy profile and stone, bring to mind what you wish to manifest. You will enjoy success when you see it. As an example, if you are working with moonstone and you want to heal an injury to your leg, imagine yourself enjoying an activity that you would be required to be at your best to do, such as dancing, running, or martial arts.

2. By putting crystals in the sun, they will naturally be recharged with the sun's energy. The sun is the source of all energy.
3. Crystals can also be recharged by the moonlight using the energy of the moon. Certain crystals are particularly connected to the moon.
4. It is also possible to recharge your crystals by placing them outside during a thunderstorm. This will use the natural energy of the storm to recharge your crystals.
5. Others choose to recharge their crystals with their breath. They do so by lying down, grounding themselves, and then breathing on their crystals several times with the intent of energizing them.
6. Running water can be used to clean crystals. This can be done under the tap at home or even better in a running stream. If you have access to a stream, you may want to place your crystals in a small net bag that you can attach to something nearby, so they won't be washed away. 24 hours would be a good period for this. Please check to see if the crystal is safe for water. (ex. Water shrinks selenite)
7. The crystal can also be placed in a basket of clear quartz for a few days. Clear quartz is a natural amplifier of energy. I highly recommend that every crystal owner have a basket of clear quartz and use it as a charging station for all crystals.

Made in the USA
Middletown, DE
04 June 2024

55303773R00038